IAN DUHIG became a full-time writer after working with homeless people for fifteen years. He has since published eight books of poetry as well as collaborating on projects with socially-marginalised groups, musicians, filmmakers and other artists. A Cholmondeley Award recipient, Fellow of the Royal Society of Literature and former International Writer Fellow at Trinity College Dublin, Duhig has won the Forward Best Poem Prize once, the National Poetry Competition twice and his *New and Selected Poems* was awarded the 2022 Hawthornden Prize for Literature.

Ian Duhig

An Arbitrary
Light Bulb

PICADOR

First published 2024 by Picador
an imprint of Pan Macmillan
The Smithson, 6 Briset Street, London EC1M 5NR
EU representative: Macmillan Publishers Ireland Ltd, 1st Floor,
The Liffey Trust Centre, 117–126 Sheriff Street Upper,
Dublin 1, DO1 YC43
Associated companies throughout the world
www.panmacmillan.com

ISBN 978-1-0350-3320-1

3 5 7 9 8 6 4 2

A CIP catalogue record for this book is available from the British Library.

Printed and bound by CPI Group (UK) Ltd, Croydon, CR0 4YY

Visit **www.picador.com** to read more about all our books
and to buy them. You will also find features, author interviews and
news of any author events, and you can sign up for e-newsletters
so that you're always first to hear about our new releases.

Contents

An Arbitrary Light Bulb

Under Sewerby Hall's Lantern of Demosthenes
I found a pebble the exact shape of a light bulb.
Then, suddenly, as if in one of my old Beanos,
another lit above my head in a thought bubble

trailing diminuendo echoes, like Little Plum's
smoke-signals, to my dull bulb of skull below
until they disappeared into that unplumbable
nothing where so many of my brainwaves go.

I sucked this stone like a pear drop in the hope
it might hatch a poem, or seed one, but, so far,
nothing worth the light, the idea's bulb blown,
an abandoned oratory that never had a prayer.

I spat it out but the hole it left was a gift to me
beyond all rhetoric to figure, or poetry to sing,
a reminder such a bulb is called an 'arbitrary' –
an arbitrary light bulb is the name of the thing.

Poem Beginning with a Line from Ashbery

'The room I entered was a dream of this room':
two dimensions, no window, wallpaper white
with black designs which moved when I slept.
The room I entered was a dream of this room.

There is another room but it is inside that one,
a tomb inside another, stanza within stanza,
poet inside poet, matryoshka matrix,
there is another room, but it is inside that one.

The theme of this room is stanza's meaning,
if meaning is more than a stain on my dream.
Old yellowed paper meant a scream of pain.
The theme of this room is stanzas dreaming.

I stayed in one room when I broke my mind.
My face grew as lined as my notebook pages.
I thought that days and poems were cages.
I didn't know the man whose name I signed.

The room I entered was a dream of this room.
That poem's dreamer lies in his, not this, tomb.
Am I an I, a you, a who or a whom?
To me, my name still seems a nom-de-plume.

Black Cat Box

I imagine my own Skinner black box
has its cat, a Pangur Dubh that chews
computer mice or scribal quills, slips
all tongues that try to call it by name

through lexical gaps a tenth of its size,
an untranslatable pun or turn of phrase,
Schrödinger nightmare, quantum of no
solace, ungraspable won't-o'-the-wisp.

It shoves me aside in this quatrain nest,
eats my poem-birds, usurps these keys
to my castle, leaves one print in snow,
wants back in: "Stuff your white space!"

It insists I have it say "There is one story
and one story only: me!" It is all poems,
abandoning us before we can finish them,
changing subjects, refusing to be subject.

I'm in a dark room looking for a black cat.
What happened to my idea for this poem?
"Talk to the paw: the puss ain't listening.
I'm thirsty now: pour me a saucer of ink!"

The Discoveries of Joash Woodrow

Returned from his National Service
in Egypt's ancient land of bondage,
Joash reorientated all his landscapes
like grid maps he made for the army.

He'd find himself inspired by fences,
collaging in sheet music so its staves
might echo the rhythm of his pickets
and the music's keys not lock him up.

Joash drew on as the nights drew in;
even in spring and summer, he drew
the blinds to work by his own lights
in the family home, his first asylum.

And the more Joash drew, the more
he withdrew, the fewer knew of him.
Few called, put off. Then all stopped.
His family left or died. He stayed on,

cannibalising furniture for sculpture,
coal sacks and cardboard for canvas.
Sectioned, he drew artistic acclaim —
and suffered the national press again.

God and the Poets

The paradox is that it is the people who think religion is prose
who keep it alive for the people who can only use it as poetry.
— Richard Holloway, *Waiting for the Last Bus*

Mass was poetry to most of my family.
At school, teachers put words into the mouths
of poets and God ("He's saying here . . .")

like the newsagent cardboard policeman's
wipeable word balloon, magic-markered
with special deals or threats to shoplifters.

If I asked about Cain's wife, Adam's navel,
or, if communion tasted like card, was Jesus
cardboard? *Smack!* teachers would explain.

Once when a visiting White Father told us
to find God not just in words but in silence,
not just in right but wrong, I was also struck.

Though I remained divided as an altar boy —
like the Hirst sheep or a magician's assistant —
when one day the newsagent wiped clean

his policeman's word balloon and left it
blank, I took it as a lesson about white spirit,
black letter law and the news that stays news.

Gaspers

After school, we'd share a 'thruppenny loosie',
its name war code, we thought: 'When England
Invaded Germany Hitler's Troops Surrendered!'
We coughed loyally. Our ex-BAOR newsagent

brought back loot, a Black Forest cigarette box
I coveted: its dispensing mechanism was a bird
which, I realised later, was the spitting image
of Professor Yaffle, the woodpecker in *Bagpuss*.

An ivory button triggered a foil-lined drawer
of Weights to open and Professor Yaffle to bow,
pluck one stiff but flimsy white worm and lift it
towards our wheezing veteran in its linden beak.

Yaffle guyed the philosopher Bertrand Russell
who professed to smoking well into his nineties
"all day except for when I'm eating or sleeping"
and that – for seventy years – it did him no harm.

Grown, I smoked untipped till my lungs crackled
like Lucozade wrappers. After his Leeds reading,
I offered MacCaig a Silk Cut. "Thank you but no:
those are just a very expensive way of breathing."

Fair Was Foul

Fair was foul, now foul is fair:
moths bred black for filthy air
bred back to white to hide again,
sun, moon, stars, rain.

Back to front and upside down
anyhow loiners built this town:
inside-out and outside in,
hearts, sleeves, inked skin.

Loiners fought with fist and kick,
stick, stone, blade, brick.
Here is hell, the poet wrote,
hellhounds nightly at his throat.

Hell's bells ting-a-ling-a-ling,
war ghost songs still echoing,
Leeds pals fell, in and out,
long, tall, short, stout;

this, that, t'other side —
anyhow next war more poor died,
anyhow more moved here to live,
sun, rain, take, give.

Moon, stars, fear, hate,
foe, friend, fight, mate;
rub down, rub out, rub up wrong
anyhow loiners rub along.

All changed, it's all the same;
getting by's the only game.
'Life is short and so is brass':
kiss me quick or kiss my arse.

Piseog on a Poet

My uncle taught me all about the piseogs,
our old Irish country spells of vengeance:
the straw halter drawn along a boundary,
a last harvest sheaf made a cailleach doll.

I could have worked with any of these:
Pegasus unbridled from you and bolted;
a barley mannequin all your readership;
the pitying pals: "He had such promise!"

But for you, as full of yourself as an egg,
I choose this: the burial of a white clutch
on your territory so, as they grow rotten,
your luck will too, unless you find them;

but that won't happen, being invisible on
your sterile pages, now to stay only white,
hiding huddles of your unhatched poems,
each fresh, a triumph: each now, a stinker.

Forms

i.m. Roddy Lumsden

This hare came with other forms.
Opened, it was light in his hands,
the colour of its paper or silence.

It hid well there in its winter coat,
but he knew this was a creature
legendary for its uncleanliness,

able to change sex every year,
invent new forms of intercourse,
bend the moon's fertility to its will.

So he fed it night and shadows
until others could see its prints,
its stained sheets, its true purity.

He did this as a lover and a poet,
because it was his nature to share
as the hare's to write its own love

in white ink on the snow, invisibly
but always there, for you, for him,
a page awaiting the fall of darkness.

An Arbitrary Light Bulb

The Bramhope Worm

Seven major faults at the crux
made rockfalls a constant risk,
walls struck by unlucky picks
given to spurt webs of cracks.

Men winched down air shafts
in buckets to work candle-lit,
get thirty bob a day-like-night
for twenty tons dug each shift.

Navvies cut their worm of air,
limestone-clad, a running sore
till one day, this worm turned:
twenty-four died underground.

Owners honoured the lost team
in their cemetery with a model
of the line's square-fort portal,
as if exalting what killed them.

This story bored into my brain
and tunnelled its way out again,
clad in a limestone-white space
to cut new lines in this soft face.

Production Lines

for Steve O'Shaughnessy

Minimum wage agency job, tea firm production line
feeding irregular tea bags the company bought cheap
into a machine which chews them up, spewing leaves
we trap in chests, then empty into another machine
that craps them out as standard bags. To go for a piss,
we must raise hands so a substitute can take our place.

New chests come stencilled with a lost empire's names,
some with stowaways in the foil lining: butterfly pupae.
A few hatch, rising like rags from a temple dancer's sari
on a music we cannot hear that yet baffles our machines.
But the factory is kept cold; they die in a few moments.
We sweep them up with torn wings of irregular tea bags.

I've looked up butterflies in libraries. None were so bright.
Steve reminded me the brand of that machine was *Zeus*,
reminding me in turn of Ganymede, Sisyphus, Psyche,
for I moved on from production lines long ago. My life
now is breaking open books, flattening wings of pages,
draining leaves so I can fill up new books, endlessly.

Poisoned Glens

You could leave on the bus, but if you came back on the bus . . .
    — Anonymous navvy via Ultan Cowley

I

Shut out of their hostels in daytime, I'd see navvies
in Kilburn pubs, thin men nursing stout and grudges
who conjured roll-ups one-handed, tales of muckers
gone home in American cars to retire; or were dead.

These soon too: faces red road maps, Irish horizons
behind eyes watery as the run-off from London clay
in the suits, cheap shoes and caps they'd worked in,
would be buried in. Unions shunned them at first,

their countrymen gangers betrayed them constantly —
bonuses not passed on, 'dead men' on wage rolls
so crews of fifteen had to do the work of twenty-five.
Protests drew blows from fists, boots, pick handles.

Wimpey = We Import More Paddies Every Year:
the dig by locals. Folkies sang 'The Tunnel Tigers'
though the best of these were men from Donegal,
so they suffered most, the worst, and died soonest.

Pat was crippled in one collapse: the crack of timber
then bones. From a mob, his crew became a machine,
a clockwork whirr of synchronised shovelling. Freed,
he was sacked the same hour. On the lump: no compo.

Oisín meant trouble to gangers, subcontractors, bosses:
tried to organise a union, a 'closed shop', then a strike
for holidays, wet time, sick leave, free protective gear —
he was given a choice: out on your arse or on your ear.

II

Tunnel tiger, working nights
in a forest of cage lights;
tunnel tiger's back near broke
in that jungle called The Smoke.

Tunnel tiger rips out clay,
tunnel tiger's ripped-off pay,
dirty work and dirty notes.
gangers lying in their throats.

Tunnel tiger's lost his job,
sacked for having too much gob,
blacklisted for that same crime,
on his hands now only time.

Laid off since he got a name,
can't go home poor out of shame,
can't go back without a car,
makes a half pint last an hour,

wanders smog-choked London streets,
pride a mind-forg'd manacle —
sees a bus with empty seats,
its destination: Donegal.

'Lough Derg trout grow fat and lazy',
white hares light his Poisoned Glen:
London memories growing hazy;
tunnel tiger's home again!

No. A lie. What would he do there?
Tunnel tiger hangs around,
an Oisín-after-the-Fenians stare
like pennied eyes for the underground.

The Seed of God

While the Parisian rioters tore up paving stones
to find the beach, I tore up Kilburn High Road
to find the world's media packing Keane's yard
where Mick Meaney lay under its London clay,
breaking the world record for being buried alive.

I was fourteen and delighted by Meaney's abuse
of mouthy American rival, Country Bill White,
on a live BBC link, just before *Songs of Praise*.
'Irish lout', some said. But this was '6os Kilburn
and Mick Meaney was meaning it for all of us.

Butty Sugrue was behind it, a man I'd once seen
pull a bus up Kilburn High Road with his teeth:
now he'd fixed them in his naive barman Mick
and dubbed him 'The Underground Champion'.
Butty promised immortality and Butty delivered.

He couched his press pitch in religious imagery:
Mick was 33, Christ's age when harrowing hell;
he slept in his coffin like a monk in Butty's pub
which laid on a wake, the local priest's blessing,
and a 'Last Supper' eaten to popping flashbulbs.

While Mick was invested under Keane's yard,
'The Gorgeous Gael' Jack Doyle sang hymns.
Mick rose again after threescore days and one,
brandishing a crucifix as if the sword of Christ
to a march from the London Irish Girl Pipers.

"It's called the *Seed of God*," wept his daughter,
Mary, "something that can make your heart soar,
and your eyes come alive. He would often return
to that time and place where he broke the record",
just as I unearth these memories, dust them off.

'Bachelor's Walk, In Memory'

on the occasion of its acquisition by the
National Gallery of Ireland

After that day, the King's Own Scottish Borderers
were to Dubliners the King's Own Scottish Murderers.

Sketching the scene of the massacre, Jack Yeats noticed
how street flower sellers memorialised these dead:

he'd place one at his painting's centre, a young woman
in a black shawl, her back to us, half turned to right;

she throws a rose for each lost soul in this open doorway
where their bodies fell, running from soldiers' rifle fire.

He shows red roses also stopped in flight, still to fall
on streets of Derry, Ballymurphy and New Lodge.

'The Green Fields of France'

We're driving towards Ripon
where Owen wrote 'Futility'
another May a century ago
before he returned to France.

Our own road falls between
sheets of hawthorn blossom,
as if morning snow drifted
from Wilfred Owen's poem.

At Coxwold, we'd stopped
at the Sterne museum to see
editions of *Tristram Shandy*
cut to fit a soldier's pocket.

So I think about Uncle Toby,
a blank page for Widow Wadman,
all Wilfred's unwritten poetry
falling like may on our road,

a song worming in my brain:
'For the sorrow, the suffering,
the glory, the pain, / the killing
and dying were all done in vain . . .'

Eternals

In *The Eternals* a London bus explodes
and becomes a cloud of red rose petals:
a surreal English image in many ways —
let me not count those, but Orwell's joys

in Woolworths roses' anarchic labelling:
a 'Dorothy Perkins' (white, yellow-heart),
a 'yellow' Polyantha that grew ruby red;
his double-yolker Albertine. All sixpence:

then, a pint and a half of mild, ten Players,
or 'twenty minutes of twice-breathed air'
at the flicks: say, two Pathé war newsreels,
A Canterbury Tale up to The Hand of Glory.

My Dad, ex-Irish Army, tried to recruit me
when I was young to help with his garden,
tend his Irish Fireflames, but I only cared
for fire roses exploding from guns in films.

Orwell scorned an Irish peace Dad guarded
but could come up with beautiful surprises,
like his Woolworths roses. I love his prose,
and flowers, silly films, and I miss my Dad.

The Father of Milk

Is non-toxic masculinity a paradox or a cliché you ask?
Both. Paradoxical Sterne contrived such in Toby Shandy,
the soldier who literally wouldn't hurt a fly. A soldier's son,

Sterne was born in Tipperary like my father – a marksman
in a neutral country's army, who never fired a shot in anger.
Discharging himself, he found no work at home, so left

to serve forty years in an English dairy. I'd call up Dad
in a phrase from D. H. Lawrence, 'the father of milk':
fertile bull of nurture, kind as Toby, even more dutiful.

When I let my guinea pig graze on our flag-sized lawn,
he watched, an airgun in his lap to keep cats off. Young,
he had a pet hare I now imagine suckling, not from cows,

like a witch hare, but his dispensing machine. This page
is also his milk carton: I stir in 'lusna' magic spider threads
of words with the 'lámh marbh' – but I lack white magic,

my 'dead hand' is cliché and sentimentality, my milk is still
spilled, my father is still in neutral Death's army, I call up
only his ghost. I have no words. The cat got my tongue.

Ground Gives

Bauman's Tetley lecture on his *Liquid Modernity*,
how free-floating anxiety is our condition now,
brought Heaney's 'Anything Can Happen' to mind,
its phrase 'Ground gives'. Anybody who stepped

on an icy pool, believing it strong enough to hold
their weight, discovers liquid modernity's meaning
in a gut-churning rush as knowledge swamps faith.
I felt such a churning as my ground gave way when

I first heard Seamus had died; at a loss for words
for the poet who'd been my grounding in this art,
who'd meant so much, whose solid words melted

to his soft Latin *vale*: 'Noli timere'. I can only think
of words on an Irish headstone: 'Ni bás ach ag fás',
'Not dead, but growing'. Ground gives. He gave.

Martian Fields

Rome is the capital of Yorkshire.
— Lewis Carroll, *Alice's Adventures Under Ground*

Out of its tiny mind
from sniffing silage
while crossing farms,

a stoned worm rolls
into Ronnie Duncan's
noted Stone Garden

to spot what it takes
for friezes of worms
on stelae and slabs —

reads the Latin quotes
as vermicular signals
and so dreams itself

an army marching on
its stomach, also god
of armies and farms:

then, mightier than
the warrior's sword,
a Martian poet's pen,

a new Virgil writing
of worms and the man,
the meaning of victory.

Nelson and spyglass,
it sights a snail ride
the waves of itself

by dandelion clocks
that blow away time
with parachute drops.

An old watering can,
its rose bullet-holed
is Martian ack-ack:

it aims at the heavens
sliced like a melon
by feathered swift jets.

Picket-fence sentries
remain at their posts
under bombardment:

a Spring Offensive's
slow green explosions
on a bulb-lit runway.

Troops wear olive drab,
lawn, daisy-eye buttons,
woodlouse epaulettes

and black beetle boots —
a lost tortoise shell is
both helmet and panzer.

In the reich of the worm
our place is to feed it:
'Earth is carnivorous'

says Finlay. 'Zz' snores
our worm. 'Breakfast!'
sings the early bird.

Still, Not

I have found a new enjoyment for my free time: lying in the grass.
— Kafka, *Diaries* 1916

My hearing aids perch
    over my ears' bass clefs,
plastic and metal wings,
    breath marks giving me

tinny pause to hear lost highs,
    bird music as light metal:
waxwing silver bells, bars
    of goldfinch; steel swift

cries sickling sea-blue sky
    for aeroplankton. I cut
through thick wood below
    where blackcaps flute,

a thrush practises scales
    but I'm flat. My ear bud
tendrils burrow in wormholes
    for the song of the earth,

roots music, ground bass,
    attention sharpened by a stone
I lie on. Not yet stone deaf.
    Still, not yet stone dead.

Marky

Is minic do bhris béal duine a shrón.
— Irish proverb

Watching this cormorant on the Wharfe
hold open its wings to the admiring sun,
I recall Marky Malone on his stag night
removing his silk suit jacket very slowly

to show off his Bullworker's pecs to us
and the man he'd picked out to fight —
who smartly coshed him across his beak
and swanned out of the silent public bar.

Marky flapped, half-in his jacket sleeves,
head back, gargling up blood as if he tried
to swallow a fish of pride stuck in his throat,
like a tame cormorant wearing a neck ring.

Heron the Hunter

for Vivek Narayanan

Heron stands his ground, unflinching in the rush,
scanning from between his kite-shield wings,
his head, a fist for a cinquedea dagger beak, tilts
this way, that, to triangulate, compute refractions.

If I can only get my own angling right, I'll catch
sight of this from my bus top deck front window
crossing the bridge over a weir of rainbow mists,
as if for Chapel Perilous and not Chapel Allerton.

Luckier yet, I glimpse a breakneck, flawless kill:
his raised, straightened throat seems triumphant,
crying out for a praise song, so I get busy with
heraldic research as soon as I arrive back home.

'Shitepoke' was an old name for a heron, I read,
from their reaction when flushed out by a stick;
'Shiterow' for weakling, is from 'Shite Heron' –
I wonder if the way of the bookworm is wrong.

My lean knight's quest is not quite so Quixotic,
stout in his attitude statant for my shield design,
matchlessly unmacho for a chivalric hatchment,
proud display for my guild of 'coward' weaklings.

No Song

Linton Bridge just down from the sign

DANGER   KEEP OUT   SEWAGE

fired from the Wharfe bank,
                            a wide sickle-swipe-sweep over the river accelerating

a furnace-chested zip of lapis lazuli:

                            beak blued needle, our eyes, hooks, catch zilch:

it's here now,

                            now

                                                    there,

now: hidden in a green shade, a darkened cinema, absorbed in the film
    of the river:

nothing, nothing, nothing, nothing, nothing

                            till

                            a flicker of gas extinguishes itself

then: an oil slick quick lit explodes the prism of water, spillage of jewels
    & is gone.

        'The modern binomial name derives from Halcyon and Atthis,
    the latter a beautiful woman and a favourite of Sappho', I read out,

'It doesn't have a song,' I add.
"It doesn't need one," she replied.

Bitterning

Like Butoh, bitterning:
how, at a threat sensed,
a spooked bird twists,
breaking its silhouette;

cryptic plumage crazes
like a dazzle ship, pose
frozen into a stalagmite
of jagged feathers, zeds.

Today, death passes by,
so the bittern unruffles
a svelte curvilinear self
from its sawtooth body.

In the corner of my eye,
I see my maker circling,
the beak of his pen set
to disject my members.

Pheasant's Eye

'A poem is a pheasant', Wallace Stevens wrote:
it makes footprints like time's arrows pointing
backwards, from here to those I once followed
over new snow till they suddenly stopped dead.

Fox? No foxprints. Thought fox then? I stared
at the blank page of this field so long, it grew
as foxed as I with patches where bulbs stirred,
preparing to happen or not, unmade by poetry.

What I don't know about pheasants would fill
a Borgesian library. Take down any book: open
it randomly; see the ghost of the nothing not
there and the nothing that is, the white sheet

a picnic cloth over bulbs of Narcissus poeticus,
the poet's Narcissus, known as pheasant's eye.

Magpied

It has also been said that the magpie was the only bird not to enter
Noah's Ark, instead deciding to sit on the roof and swear
at the drowning world
– Andrew Millham, *Singing Like Larks*

Football-rattle cackle,
Gazza in Italian
and Newcastle

mocks the kit
of good and evil,
day and night,

life and death;
dove and crow
jammed together.

Coming unstuck,
its motley reflects
this page's palette,

poetry's yin-yang
sex of language
and silence. But

[32]

more truly it is high-
tackle hues, bruise-
purple, green, blue.

In lore, its tongue
hid Devil's blood,
just a drop. Poetry.

Auk Roosting

Auk sounds like how it goes
and its direction: awkward,
flying or walking. But water
is a language an auk knows

backwards, sideways, forwards,
its own tongue untelling the tails
of fish which are water's words
to sing their descending scales.

This auk is black and white,
a little red – like my poetry,
you said – yet it's hard to write:
I'm unauklike when all at sea,

liker one on land, and as for air,
my poems do so struggle there
they could even pass for auks.
One roosted here. Now it talks.

Toad Poetry

Why should I let the toad 'poetry'
    squat on my life?
I could write like this, just prosy
    simple stuff

that won't take a whole year to grow
    like some flower. Arse!
I see flowers through the bus window
    when I pass:

in no imaginary municipal garden,
    they're real as toads
but don't find blossoming a burden,
    nor eat words.

Folk struggle to buy their family
    enough to eat:
I'm lucky to be writing anything.
    Words are cheap.

Yet something poetic and unkillable
    still fuels my soul,
firing me to find the run of the mill
    beautiful,

like bird song I know means "Stuff off!"
    or "Stuff me!"
(the latter at bottom still the stuff of
    poetry).

Dogshit too, blossoming by birds
    on bush and branch,
the black plastic seed case spreads
    its high stench;

even such can flower bright words
    in good time:
not just in Hull are toads and turds
    a full rhyme.

Dents-de-Lion

for Jane

For Marvell's four hundredth anniversary,
and our fortieth, driving to Nun Appleton
we'd find our world locked out, the estate
invested in ruination by some new owner.

Coming back, we turned at a gate opening
onto a field plush with dandelions in seed,
hazy Belisha beacons shedding white hair.
We stopped to see clocks shower soft fluff

into May air and birdsong, blowing over
iron gates and chain-link fences, leaving
pads on stalks like buttons on green foils.

Sweetness, let us hold each other and roll
in our quilt until it bursts like a blowball,
while we may, while our own roads allow.

Ruby Anniversary

Dining out for their anniversary,
they waited for a table: at the bar,
rowing about lateness, an old war,
a cold war: the peace too was icy.

So the barman invited the couple
to watch a trick of his for a laugh:
he pushed an empty shot glass up
to its brim into a half-empty, half-

full Guinness and had them draw
closer until, in sunlight, they saw
the meniscus ring was ruby, what
seemed black and white, was not.

Bederoll

Sing now of Ravenser Odd, Hrafn's Eyr,
'Raven's Tongue' in old Viking speech;
once as big as Hull it was lost to a storm
called 'Grote Mandrenke' in Low Saxon,
which means the Great Man-drowning'.

North Sea tongues have licked this coast
clean of all French out of Sand le Mere;
Northorpe nor Ravenspur were spared;
Hyde's hidden along with the holy Latin
of Sisterkirke, Monkwell and Monkwike.

Waxholme melted, Dimlington dimmed,
Ringborough is ripples, Out Newton out,
cold all old landholders of Colden Parva,
Withow, Owthorne drowned with howls:
a bederoll of ghosts, their graves all water.

A Picnic

At first almost nothing:
an inkling of porcelain
as from a wind-chime,
then, the breakers crash,

windows web and give,
splintering to rainbows,
the sockets fizz and pop
and shelves pour books.

Outside, lawns slump,
drunk, and are gone,
apple trees are thrown
like brides' bouquets.

The cliff tears inland,
clawing down fields,
fences, cows, streets,
pillows of rainclouds.

Suddenly its huge roar
is drowned by silence,
clothes don't flap now,
here, fathoming . . .

The tablecloth trick
reverses in thick air
settling for a picnic
in the kelp forest.

A saucer see-saws
down this way, that,
to catch the teacup,
gathering this storm.

Contrary

You have to be free to play around with the notion that day might be night, love might be hate; nothing can be too sacred for the imagination to turn into its opposite.
— Adrienne Rich

'Sdrawkcab' explains the novelist on Facebook,
describing a technical angle of his address
to the themes in his new book.

There, he writes how he hears
Yorkshire as 'dhearcadh siar', the Irish for
'a backwards look', and how the county boasts

of being the final home of great sean-nós singer,
Darach Ó Catháin. My home too a half-
century, our contrary Leeds, which another book

called *The Back-to-Front, Inside-Out, Upside-
Down City* as if some Bach fugue, its name,
like Bach, also an echo of the Welsh,

some say – 'lloed', in English 'a place',
which gives nothing away, as its locals do
to strangers who ask them too many questions.

'A place in love with roads', writes the novelist,
quoting me. Navvies like Darach helped lay them
for even more traffic to further blacken the air

of the blackest of white rose cities. It had a dark
side: its team adopting Real Madrid's white,
would earn the nickname 'Dirty Leeds'.

Traditionally, Leeds's left would be right,
arguments cast in terms of black and white
and everybody, everywhere else, wrong.

Yet, contrariwise, the local pronunciation
by its Tony Harrisonian [uz] of the definite article
was almost indefinite, a slight, subtle, [t] . . .

Should one loiner describe another as 'roaring',
they would not mean with joyful laughter,
but from tears. If she calls you 'Pal',

she may be preparing to batter you.
Its town chippies sell battered Creme Eggs,
as if to honour John Donne who wished his heart

would be so by his 'three-person'd God',
as though He was a kind of cannibal loiner deity.
But this city did frighten incoming poets,

its men ready to bray you over a sidelong look.
Even Leeds's red ranks of back-to-backs
seemed set for duelling with pistols.

Do I sound like I dislike this city?
Not to those who know: I show my love
truly, rightly, deeply Leeds-like: sdrawkcab.

Blocks

In Martin Bell's poem 'Writer's Block',
he figures his own as 'furniture of hell
. . . an elaborate machine of twisting,
gleaming parts hewn from solid metal'.

Firstly, admire Bell's professionalism:
a poem hewn from inability to write;
block as tool chest, his legerdemain
I am here to learn from, stuck myself.

This mirror-trick turns writer's block
to desk, uncut new book, magic box
with contents we imagine into being:
barded and trapped, an auto-Pegasus.

A better name might be 'Engine Block'
where 'furniture' means needed gear,
a well-equipped workshop fit to make
nothing happen on an industrial scale.

I choked before I started this, ignition
being achieved with Bell's jump leads,
though he's dead, that poets' paradox:
good ones passing, yet always with us.

The Point

*Poems, if they were buses, should have
'unknown destination' on the front.*
— Mona Arshi

The point of a bus is windows, for Laird:
a top front-seat view an image for poetry.
What you see from up here, cars cannot:
over hedges or Enclosure dry stone walls,

Yorkshire rising again in the slow motion
of isostatic rebound from ancient glaciers,
all time melting into limestone landscapes,
clints and grykes, Auden's cracking lines.

Sometimes, a bus stops for no passengers,
only so a timetable can catch itself up,
that its nets of numbers seem thrown over
the real world, like longitude and latitude.

They wait too to be Ravilious's gutted hull,
open-topped, its passengers only weather,
windows wind-eyes. The point of the bus
is that it stops — like life, as Kafka wrote;

the poem, for Simic, is a clock designed
to do just that, the poet its passing maker,
a ticking lyric I. My ghost in this machine
is smiling at you from the top deck window.

Omni

William Barnes proposed that we call buses
'folkswains', which sounds folk kitsch, or even völkisch.
'Bus' has stuck, from 'omnibus': 'for all',
for [uz] – kin to 'omnium-gatherum',
a ragbag, like Leeds and this offcuts bin
of labyrinthine thoughts from my home since
its 'Motorway City' days – a maze then,
but *the* place to get your fancy threads made.
No more: our rag trade's gone for a Burton,
that phrase from Leeds terse speech which Harrison
thought fell naturally in blank verse lines –
which term suits me fine: my mind's often blank;
I'll lose the thread, bear no comparison
with Calvino's Ersilians whose own threads
wound through city streets to indicate
relationships with colour-coded clues,
so weave their state into a life-size text
of unity until, too tied, they'd leave
to found their next Ersilia elsewhere.
The UK's 'imagined community'
has nowhere else: it snapped the threads that mapped
its maze and got lost following a bus
with lies along its side. In sympathy,
I'll dérive via bus from town to town.
This line aspires to 'libraries' –
in truth a shelf on which I leave a Sterne
then glimpse in passing that blue civic plaque

for great folk musicologist Frank Kitson.
Opposite, Des Hurley told me once
in the Irish music pub, The Roscoe,
that Leeds's local fiddle-playing styles
were influenced by rhythms of the mills.
From town I reel back out to Wetherby
while looking for the Huguenot arch carved
'Aimez votre prochain comme vous-même'
(the Sun King exiled them). I could say too,
'L'état, c'est moi' for my state, all at sea.
Our pasts are not the pasts we've long been sold.
Old Huguenots could train us to reweave
the national tapestry, tie in rogue threads,
not hide a stain but set it in the pattern —
but that, today, is just too rational.
The suit the last Leeds tailor should now sell's
the kind that comes with matching cap and bells.

Histories

Valkyries sang as they wove bloody doom
for the Irish fighting the Norse at Clontarf:
their woof was guts, warp-weights skulls,
for reels, red arrows, swords their shuttles.

Scott noted this song heard 'in the Norse'
among Orcadians the same year Gott built
his mill where Norse spiked local dialects.
The Irish were cursed in it, there, for sloth,

dozy at looms, so no Valkyrie need sing
for the woof to snap, the bolts to redden.
In cobbled lanes, the barefoot incomers
fought locals in clogs rimmed with iron.

Now it's Morris dancers wear clog-irons,
an up-and-downer is a verbal argument;
that mill is the city's Industrial Museum
celebrating multicultural work heritage.

Valkyries sang Clontarf's wrong victors,
wove flesh clothes for ghostly emperors.
Poems can be noisy looms spinning lines:
a mill girl signs to you, over this one's din.

Portrait of the Artist as a Young Offender

In prison, Tom lifted poems
from 'In Memoriam' columns,
flogging them to fellow cons
for letters to their loved ones

to show their personal growth,
the softer side they'd developed –
the greater sense of self-worth,
by joining a poetry workshop.

Then Tom noticed, to his horror,
poems in the papers recur,
altered only in their names . . .
If supply gave him problems,

demand had grown rampant
with his customers not men
it was healthy to disappoint.
He paused. He lifted his pen.

Sausage of Death

A Danish idiom for the painfully boring —
waiting room *Reader's Digest* indigestion
from editions well past their use-by dates,
sick-bed TV, golf or an unfinished poem

stuck in the wit's colon like a wrong skin,
made with wrong cuts and without stock,
the concentration in what was to Walcott,
'the essential cube that really is the poem'.

Square, skinless, an Argyll Lorne sausage
slices into red pages like teenagers' poems
but life was sausage of death to Berryman,
even literature. Especially Great Literature.

I'm more a Dieter Roth *Literaturwurst*,
tied off at each end, stuffed in between,
painfully bored by forks in frying pans,
on fires, bored to death, then in hell too.

Internal Border

In the end it is the same. Singing, and silence.
— Janáček, *The Makropulos Case*

Music happens between the notes,
Yo-Yo Ma is supposed to have said,
for Debussy, in the space between:
the same idea with different accents.

At a reading, I heard Holub apologise
for his heavy Czechoslovakian accent:
"Soon, it will only be a Czech accent,
but even so, you won't understand it."

'Kolik řečí umíš, tolikrát jsi člověkem'
explains a Czech proverb I cannot say,
which means, 'You are as many times
a person as the languages you can speak'.

At the border of my new self, the guard
who wears my face speaks a language
I cannot understand, will ask for my ID.
I will sing instead, and he will shoot me.

Irrgarten

If life had a second edition, how I would correct the proofs.
— John Clare

Error Garden, German: 'maze',
all the errors of my ways,
all my errors in a garden,
all my errors and no pardon.

Left school early, first wrong turn,
manual jobs but studied nights;
found another way to learn
in the dark by other lights.

Bored by university,
I worked with homeless people next;
got some writing poetry,
mazy city streets our text.

Project closed, I turned to verse,
workshops, teaching, fellowships;
cups and sups and lips and slips,
little money in my purse.

From dirty hands to dirty looks
not a turn up for the books.
For those I loved, still harder times:
I tried to bind myself with rhymes.

My second little brother died,
I turned to dope, more pills and drink:
'childhood trauma!' doctors sighed.
This way swim or that way sink.

Twice up, twice down, nearly drowned:
saved by love, things turned around.
Do demons still lurk round the bend?
Yes. Where each line meets its end.

Error gardens, all dead ends,
error gardens, most lines crossed,
error gardens host my lost:
family, lovers, poets, friends.

Error gardens I've since built:
walls of lies and walls of guilt.
Being lost feels so like home,
so like being in this poem.

Deathwatch

I thought being old was child's play,
no more painful than grey hair;
"It's nothing," Dad would wince and say.
Perhaps he knew I didn't care.

Dad's age when he died, I've long known
how wrong I was: joints swell and twist
at knee and ankle, shoulder, wrist
where raw bone grinds against raw bone.

Like him, I'll hide pain, face as ashen,
pretend I bend to tie my shoe.
Now bowels don't suggest compassion:
bloody flare-ups strip their screw

as IBD, COPD
join OCD – yet nerves feel free
and fit to highlight every pain.
But memories cloud, names fall like rain.

All his family who'd died
would slip my older brother's mind
till prompted by the dim-but-kind.
I can't forget the way he cried.

Mnemonic more than lyrical,
rhyme's how I wind my way through age,
science's great miracle:
prolonging life in its worst stage.

The deathwatch in me rocks and ticks,
a tethered beetle's spellbound tread
around its twisting maze of thread
and, like my twisting bones, it clicks.

Concertina wheeze of lung,
labyrinthine cramp-struck guts,
unwinding mind . . . no ifs, no buts,
I'm only glad that I'm not young.

Michael Longley Reads 'Harmonica'

A light in sound, a sound-like power in light . . .
Where the breeze warbles, and the mute still air
Is Music slumbering on her instrument.
— S. T. Coleridge, 'The Eolian Harp'

He tells us first of the time he brought home a harmonica
and was surprised his father played it so well, a talent
acquired in the trenches, where he played it for his men.

'My dad like old Anaximenes breathes in and out . . .'
As he begins, I recall one event review which described
my own reading voice as 'like a broken harmonica . . .'

The bruised reeds of my vocal cords now suck in the air
Anaximenes breathed out to say, it is the air holding us
and our world together: Michael, his father, the men

his poem laments with its 'orchestra of harmonicas'.
The poem's like blues, whose players call harmonicas
mouth harps. I hear one accompanying a heavenly choir

of Tommies and Fritzs who sing 'Stille Nacht, holy night'
together, beyond any language, their breath becoming
a pure air they follow into the music of eternal light.

My dark croak is harmonising by its merciful silence
where I'm a corbie as the cortège passes under my tree,
the wind playing its branches like a harp's broken strings.

An Aroko for David Oluwale

1930–1969

Oluwale is Yoruba for 'God has come home'
but he came to find hell in God's Own County,
no home but cold Leeds streets or police cells,
in his asylum only electroconvulsive therapy.

Now by the Aire, where David drowned fleeing
policemen's boots, his feet light from hunger,
my small nomadic cowrie garden grows for one
who'd grown to be a shell of himself in this city.

An empty cowrie is full as an egg with meanings:
Gods' eyes, they make arokos, magic messages.
Because efa, Yoruba for six, has the same letters
as the word to draw, my six cowries set down here

draw David's Christian ghost into Oshun's arms,
water Goddess with a name of water, that he too
might step into the true meaning of his name,
borne back to Africa where the river of us all rose.

This alchemy of cold fire on the Aire's earth makes
nothing happen, like poetry, yet makes something
from nothing for a man treated like he was nothing,
making room to reflect on river water running softly.

Forced

Labouring in Hepworth's cloth warehouse
fifty years ago, I met one of David's killers:
ex-cop ex-con security man, drunken bully
we scorned for his soft time then softer job.

'The Cloth' local cops called their uniform
but also meaning the vocation. Their force
was wound up that same year, 'The Cloth'
rendered down as shoddy from such shame.

David's story threaded through my life since,
drew me into homelessness work, winding
through my poems: often with two left feet,
but there are worse things than willed verse.

I read some at the installation of his plaque
on Leeds Bridge just above the spot where
those cops forced him into the Aire to drown.
Its new bridge is also named for Oluwale,

a fit symbol of this city, connecting itself
to itself like a poem; who we want to be
with who we were; bad to good, right to
wrong, from left to right then back again

like the shuttles that wove Leeds's wealth,
or, for me, light veering across this page,
turning white to black, silences to words.
The plaque was torn down within hours,

its replacement as fast but most in this city
united for him, posting copies of the plaque
all over Leeds: high over its busiest roads,
in Kirkgate Market, outside the Playhouse.

Sticky replicas were made, given away free,
mailed off to our more distant well-wishers.
His story raged through social media; local
and national newspapers ran it, the BBC, ITV.

'St David' an old BNP blog sneered I recall;
well maybe this was St David's first miracle:
who'd vilify him and us became the vilified,
who'd erase him now his greatest publicists,

shade they sought to throw grew sweetness,
as Yorkshire rhubarb forced from darkness,
as David's story sought the light, the bridge
between us this air we will walk on, always.

Cecilia Vicuña's *Word & Thread*

Her *Quipo* sculptures reinterpret Andean knotted cords
recording data: 'A word carries another word as thread
searches for thread. A word is pregnant with other words
and a thread contains other threads'. In this poem, Vicuña

weaves in etymologies so, buying it from Alec Finlay's
Gaza medical fundraiser, I thought, is gauze from 'Gaza'
as I've heard? In the post, *Word & Thread* wound its way
to my textile city. Rapt, I type out lines to feel them run

through my fingers: 'Thread feels the hand as the word
feels the tongue . . . movements of the fibre should be in
opposition.' My thread runs by Victor Jara, whose strings
wove songs of opposition, killed in a stadium tunnel maze,

to Gaza's innocents lost in asymmetric wars of minotaurs,
its maze with no saving threads but those in woven gauze.

Flashes

Dead as the light
bulb is living still
— David Shapiro, 'Light Bulb'

On a school seaside holiday, I stumbled upon
a shiny patch of beach; 'it's *shocked quartz*'
a teacher explained, 'or *fossilised lightning*'.
I was shocked too, to know of such a change,

that bolt-struck sand fizzed to crazy mirrors,
as if my souvenir Alum Bay glass egg-timer
could turn in a flash to infinity-looped bulbs
cracking at views of past, present and future:

of my love, her hair sunrise round her head;
of my shocked boy born under electric sun;
of a bald man, glasses like a bent egg-timer,
conducting these lines here from his Cloud,

soon unknowing why pads shock his chest,
the meaning of what flashes before his eyes
or that cloud over the crematorium chimney
without lightning: then why nothing shines.

My Friends

a departure from Lorca's 'Desde Aqui'

this is just to say,
among other things,

I'm dead. Water sings
where willows sway —

still, I have died.
But my eyes

will remain wide
under the sky's

paper tissue,
and, if a ghost,

what star I go to,
I go to with no host.

Notes

p.1 An 'arbitrary' light bulb is the most common design, frequently seen in old comic books appearing over a character's head when they have a good idea.

p.3 'Black Cat Box' alludes to the black box metaphor of Skinnerian behaviourists for the unobservable thoughts and feelings of a mind, to the more general scientific 'black cat analogy' and to the ninth-century Irish poem 'Pangur Bán' ('White Pangur'). 'Pangur Dubh' means 'Black Pangur'.

p.4 'The Discoveries of Joash Woodrow' was inspired by the reclusive Leeds artist. His considerable oeuvre became known to the art world after a fire at his home, where he lived alone at seventy-seven, led to his compulsory hospitalisation as a danger to himself. Woodrow's story and the quality of his art attracted national press attention, including from *The Times*, *The Sunday Times* and *The Spectator*. Various exhibitions of his work were mounted and he is now represented in several major international collections.

p.7 'Fair Was Foul' is a localised mash-up of the witches' chant in *Macbeth* and E. E. Cummings' 'anyone lived in pretty how town'. Verse 3 refers to Martin Bell's line in his 'The City of Dreadful Something': 'Why, Leeds is Hell, nor am I out of it'. Verse 7 translates a quotation from Macheath in Brecht's *Threepenny Opera:* 'Das Leben ist kurz und das Geld ist knapp' – also the motto of a German budget supermarket in Leeds, I've been told, although I have been unable to confirm which one.

p.9 My uncle Tommy Duhig did indeed tell me about piseogs and wrote up our local folklore for archives like Meitheal Dúchas. His contributions can now be read on their website, including one about the 'dead hand' ('lámh marbh'), a spell mentioned in 'The Father of Milk', p.21.

p.10 'Forms': although I didn't find this out until much later, when I sent my poem 'The Lammas Hireling' in for a competition, it was in a copy so pale it could have been rejected. Roddy Lumsden was helping with admin and took the trouble to re-photocopy it, drawing out print contrast to make it more legible for the judges. A marvellous poet himself, Roddy is remembered by many people with gratitude, admiration and affection.

p.13 'Poisoned Glens': the title of this poem alludes to that beautiful part of Donegal, the Poisoned Glen. 'On the lump' was construction slang for being employed without paying tax and N.I. and 'compo' meant compensation. The first line of the second-last verse quotes Ewan MacColl's song 'The Tunnel Tigers', following verses that echo Blake's 'Tyger, Tyger' and 'London'. The Irish expression 'Oisín i ndiaidh na bhFiann' ('Oisín after the Fenians') means to be alone in the world, the last of your kind.

p.19 'The Green Fields of France' quotes from Eric Bogle's song of that name.

p.21 'The Father of Milk': although my Uncle Tommy was coy about how a lámh marbh might be obtained, folklorist Joe Flanagan of Lough Cutra, interviewed on RTÉ, said that it was relatively easy to cut the hand off a corpse at a wake and smuggle it away unnoticed as so much drink would be taken on these occasions, the watchfulness of those present would be hindered.

p.27 'Marky': the Irish proverb epigraph translates as 'It is often a man's mouth broke his nose.'

p.28 'Heron the Hunter': Vivek Narayan helped me with the etymologies in this poem and also explained that the heron is a key symbol in the ancient Tamil poetry he was engaged in translating at the time. 'Coward' is a heraldic term for one of the placements of the tail.

p.30 The last line of 'Bitterning' alludes to Horace's phrase 'disjecta membra poetae' ('the limbs of a dismembered poet') from his *Satires* I. 4. 62.

p.42 'Contrary': The novelist referred to is David Wheatley, well known as an award-winning poet but then was commenting on his 2022 debut novel *Stretto*, which I also recommend. I am further indebted to David for his help with the Irish in this book.

p.45 'Blocks': Martin Bell moved to Leeds in 1967 to take up a Gregory Fellowship and stayed here until his death in 1978, the same year that the poet John Riley was killed in the sort of casual violence that so haunted Bell and his poems such as 'The City of Dreadful Something', alluded to in 'Fair Was Foul'.

p.46 The Eric Ravilious work referred to in 'The Point' is his 1934 watercolour 'No. 29 Bus'.

p.49 This Valkyries' episode in 'Histories' is taken from the skaldic poem *Darraðarljóð* in chapter 157 of *Njál's Saga*.

p.53 The epigraph is from one of Clare's letters quoted by J. W. and A. Tibble in *John Clare: A Life*, OUP, 1932.

p.59 'Forced' was written to be read at the reinstallation of a Leeds Civic Trust plaque in David Oluwale's memory on Leeds Bridge near where he drowned. The title alludes to, among other things, the favoured local method of growing rhubarb, 'forcing', which involves placing the plants in dark, heated sheds to encourage their growth as they seek the light of the sun.

p.61 'Cecilia Vicuña's *Word & Thread*'. The etymology for gauze alluded to in this poem, although widely cited, is open to question. Wiki suggests that it more probably derives from Persian gazi, a thin cloth or Arabic qaz, raw silk.

Acknowledgements

I am grateful to the editors of the following where some of these poems, or versions of them, first appeared: *Bcd Lilies*, *Blackbox Manifold*, *The Irish Times* website, *Poetry Ireland Review*, *Poetry London*, *Poetry Salzburg Review*, *Poetry Wales*, *Raceme*, *Strix* (Leeds), *The Dark Horse*, *The London Magazine*, *The North*, *The Poetry Review*, *The Stinging Fly*, *The Times Literary Supplement*, *We're All In It Together: Poems for a Disunited Kingdom*, edited by Kayleigh Campbell, Steve Ely and Michael Stewart (Grist Books, 2021), *Weston, a necessary dream*, a book celebrating Ronnie Duncan's stone garden on the occasion of his ninetieth birthday, edited and published by Polly Feversham and Diane Howse, 2018.

Many hands made this light work but I am especially grateful to my editor, Colette Bryce, who helped me untangle the wiring maze of my manuscript and see new connections. The remaining errors are entirely mine.

When I'm going into my final box,
that verse with breath of faux oak
where all shades of meaning wait
as plotlines in overwound clocks;
before my life's gone up in smoke,
asked if I'd rewind this same fate
I'd say yes, for half such love, yes
for a fifth, for a tenth, for far less.